9

m
mp
Pat

The Glass Adonis

The Glass Adonis

C. A. TRYPANIS

CHILMARK PRESS
New York

Library of Congress Catalog Card Number 72-96919

ISBN: 394-48571-8

Printed in Great Britain

To Victor

Contents

ACKNOWLEDGEMENT

The Chilmark Press of New York published a
limited edition of *The Elegies of a Glass Adonis,*
and some of the other poems included in this book
appeared on the Editorial Page of *The New York
Times.*

Memory Killed

The leaves falling and the hard blue hills
naked to the sea, gold brown russeted
jag-edged leaves fall,
we cannot touch what has fallen once
into the silence of the island wind, the
second touch, of death.

Now everything is drifting down
jag-edged russeted brown
into that other light you must not touch,
the second touch, death's.

Fingers of sun, the black-hatched bees
the swish of white bellies, swallows,
they live in the falling leaves,
if longing fingers do not touch them
drifting gold-sided russet-tipped
into the silence of the island wind
behind the humming roofs of island houses
on to the stone of that ripe church,
when naked hills rise
hard in the salt light—
today everything drifts down.

Theatre of Thasos

Come,
for the Thracian thunderstorm is rolling
to the South, the wind is tuning up
the terror of his song,

come,
for the fury of that shapeless dance
is wasting all the dazzle of its rage,
only what flesh can feel is true,
Orestes, Orestes.

This theatre overgrown by leafless wood
facing the tragic blue of winter water,
this helpless tempest begs you
give her back the power
to ripen into cruelty her rage;

without your feeble flesh,
Orestes, Orestes,
the Furies cannot tread the empty stage.

Symeon the Mystic

He saw that inner light blossoming fast,
a hungry star thorning the East,
then like the full-moon cutting through the night
and then the breaking sun drowning his heart,
drowning his cell,
a storm of dazzled whiteness.
Younger that almond-blossom swung his heart,
the flesh, a rush of love to join his God—
an ancient mystic in an ancient cell.

Under October trees hung with cool
silence I saw that light,
soft amber star-streaks, golden like the moon
then files of flame ripped from the fall of Troy.
The glowing leaves came gushing through the eyes,
' the heart, the limbs,
a silent fusion with that god of wood!

No slinking nymph, no horned shape,
no voice, no wash of wing, no stealthy hare,
silence,
only that dawn of leaves upon the air,
only that storm of gold drowning the heart
and memories of trees,
the sighs of long forgotten lovers
who carved initials on the bark,
touch of pink blossom on the cracking wood,
the feel of painted birds,

longings
for wood that travelled through the misty seas
to dry white sails in harbours of the East
where sun-baked sailors smoke and wait and talk,
logs in a leaping fire, ashes, smoke,
crosses, crucified crosses,
where cross and hanging flesh are one.

And then
the broken sky had slammed its door of cloud.
I stood
with neither god nor flesh nor hope nor wood,
October scowling through the turning leaves
that hung dead staring in a crown of blood.
Such moments never last and never die.

Edfou

It was not the giant pylon, the lettered walls,
cobra-crowned kings and priests, bitter-beaked hawks,
captives crippled in supplication
or the lion-headed goddess that moved me.

It was the few roughly scratched names near the roof
of that heavy-pillared temple—Legere, Mabilat,
Ruellet, Roland—soldiers Napoleon had flung
to this fringe of the desert
in one of his trances for power.

Billeted here in that sanded-up temple of horror,
cut off from all they had known, had loved,
what mirage of orchards, cool tapering trees,
fair-headed women of France had filled their eyes
as they gazed on those passionate sunsets
to the green dirge of the Nile.

Tall dreams of Empire, what endless hours
of boredom and longing, harder than sickness and death,
you drag in your trail—Legere, Mabilat, Ruellet, Roland,
names forgotten, obscurer than those tangled hieroglyphics,
much nearer the heart.

Desert Sunset

What anger of the desert burns
  in that crushed amber light,
  what curse of immortality, plight
  harder than granite when night returns.

O humble Coptic Christ,
  take pity on that lettered waste
  of arrogance, that taste
  of dust in mouths once richly spiced,

Release
  their golden mummy-bands of pride,
  in your compassion guide
  those searching blue enamelled birds to peace.

A Mummy's Prayer

The desert stretches out in copper rust,
star-blossoms travel in the river's stream,
my mouth is bitter with the taste of dust,
my eyes too dry to dream.

Alight upon this gold-encrusted breast,
fold your enamel wings
under the lettered scarab, rest,
for darkness brings

Jackal and robber to the gleam of gold,
give me but one more night
to lie among my toys these tomb-walls hold,
take flight,

when in the East you see the green day break
flooding the waking trees with living light—
return, enamelled bird, do not forsake
this dust-dry frame to-night.

Farewell Agathocles

'Farewell, Agathocles.'
I greet on your behalf the trees
of Attica, I touch upon her earth
your touch, the footprints of your
hound, still turning to see
lest you have stepped out
of the stone, leaving him
there alone.

'Farewell, Agathocles',
your dreams a wisp of cloud,
but still your limbs,
firm in their youth, explain
the grief that froze
into that stone 'farewell'.

Telos

Erinna, Erinna here on this beach,
these foam-noosed rocks, I call on you,
a voice long lost, the friend you mourned,
that childhood spun in a distaff,
catch-me-turtle, dolls,
the wedding torches, death.

In the East those haughty kings
were building pillared cities,
they fought, they fell,
but did not touch your life;
for only what is near is true
and what is true will live.

Erinna, Erinna, on this rocky
beach I call on you.

The Garden Wall

My childhood walks—always that wall,
that iron gate well-barred,
behind it tall
black cypresses standing on guard.

Yellow grass had stuffed the jaw
of the lion-head knocker, its handle gone.
Who was the last to cross that door,
those steps of freckled stone?

Since then it glooms a ghost-door locked,
a garden wall that seems
to keep the taut eyes always blocked
from flowers and first dreams.

Eugenie

I heard your voice beyond
the reach of silence,
that imprint of muscles on the sand
brought the taste of rain to my lips
in a morning stripped of shadows.

Sand-lilies swing across the beach,
a breath of honey rides upon the wind,
but all I see are eyes watching
the skyline, where flutter of sails
meets the flutter of wings.

Ejüp

Suburb of cemeteries,
turbaned stones
where the blind light
of great mosques is burning,
what feast of suffering,
unanswered longing
leaps in those eyes?

Ageing women,
crooked by the load
of poverty and years,
of long hopes dead,
ancient regrets
sharp as the pointed minarets
cut in the silent sky
when the sun
smouldering sets.

Zum Dank der wiederkehrten Söne

(Inscription on a large wooden cross near the
door of the church of Our Lady at Andechs)

For Erni Beck

Only The Mother whose numb hand
had stumbled once across
the flesh dragged off the Holy Cross
could understand,
pity a mother dumb
with grief, dumb with despair,
whose thoughts, dark ivy, clung to prayer,
and shield her sons from howling shell and bomb.

What if those sons returned to find a world
of swelling rubble, flattened dreams,
what if the screams
of soldiers hurled
into a death of ice and steel hung in their ears?
Whiter than apple-blossom in the spring
their mother saw them bring
the happy tears.

She took the cross, as promised, on her back
and drudged the long road to the holy shrine,
symbol huge and martyrical to shine
across the centuries, black

23

eroded letters telling the trees above,
the fields below,
to those still innocent, to those who know:
'A mother's is the widest love.'

Northern Christ

Northern Christ,
child of frost and rain
your firm lips iced
never complain.

The forehead creased
speaks for the mouth,
shaming the sharp-tongued East
the loud-voiced South.

Paregoritissa
Arta 1944

Those swallows built their nests
under the stern eyes of prophets,
near angels and saints
who have forgotten how to laugh—
neither glass nor wood
keep out the rain.

They fly across the torn mosaic
where Adam's scull splashed with glass blood
gapes at their twittering beaks,
and Eve still silently calls: 'Rise, Adam,
from your sleep that equals death,
I hear the swallows singing' . . . .

Roman Crucifixion

But not like Him—the dust whirled in the Roman
sunset, the ragged leaves dropped to the sky,
the divers scorned.

Daybreak, the sound of oars across a lake,
nets, nets with sun-red fish, the nets of words:
'Thou shalt stretch forth thy hands'. . . .

Is there but one crucifixion?
Did a cock cry three times
as the blood burst on his ears?

Byzantine Crucifixion

The occasion is grand and tragic,
women are weeping, the men stand
silent, the sky is black,
darker than the shadow of the cross.

There He stands alone on the fringe of utter
silence, though a huge crowd is staring,
because death—even His death—
is a private affair.

But my heart, faithless, goes out
to those two little angels
who cling to their eyes in horror,
—the purest childish horror—
at such an incredible sight.

Chicago Starlings

City starlings—they never leave,
though the summer is dead
and leaves peep through snow-drifts
and the thrown crumbs of bread
are few.
The sharp wind numbs their wings,
yet here they stay,
afraid of those who feed them
and afraid to fly away.

The Weather-Cock

Below me in the gabled square
Men chatter, bargain, quarrel, love,
I never stoop to watch or share
The village gossip, far above

I stand on guard ruling the sky
And neither snow nor sideway rain
Nor zig-zagged thunder, though they try,
Scare me or dent my bronze disdain.

Men call it spineless, sly to turn
With every wind that heightens pace,
If they looked closer they would learn
I swirl to meet storms face to face.

Against the blue, against the grey
I watch unruffled every light
Hailing the mounting sun good-day,
Bidding the dropping moon good-night.

To Rania

The Elegies of a Glass Adonis

I

FIRST VOICE
—We were not told they had been wrecked, only we heard their
    voices
in dry wells of villages behind grey churches
in the cry of rust-splashed birds—wood water-ripe
blacker than rotting fruit, hulks hugged by tangled weeds
where time flows like the shadow of a fish,
cold poise of throats snatches of limbs
stone shimmering through corpse-green slime
eyes water-worn, the lips salt-gnarled—
painted ships.

           We searched the sea-caves,
only the breath of ancient love stretched in their dampness
green pools of silence like a mermaid's eyes.
Memory seeps away in that long sleep of slime
where no arms reach to stroke the wounded stone.
Shreds only of green bronze cling to their rust shapes—
a boy watching a pecking bird? a man? the apple rolled out of
    his hand?
'Why,' you had said, 'must the hands of robbers
be the last flesh to touch them?'

                 Remember those gestures of limbs
when midday was swelling, lechery of light.
The hunt was over,
he lay there killed by the accurate wounds of Acteon's hounds.

C   33

Death swings an artist hand, life snapped
grows taller, clings closer to the heart.

A place there is for every shape,
those firm limbs were not made to be pitied;
now they are slime-and-weed belonging,
the star-fish and urchins have climbed into their mouths
and scratched the thinking eyes. We must live with the empty
    stones
they dimpled once so swiftly with their feet,
letters hammered backwards brushed by dry tails of lizards
in the striped silence of shadows,
white images against a dawn of glass
deep at the bottom of our eyes.
                                    Have you noticed
how the roses in the garden freeze to glass
when feather-crystals lash the winter pond
and in the birds' round stare a southern sun is burning?
Have you not noticed that the cool wings of irises
watching through broken pillars the broken gods are made of
    glass?
that in the village church nearby the wounds of that Adonis
    Christ—
oleanders anemones—stretched out on a dim gold sheet
smoulder in glass? are caught up by blanch light of candles,
the glazed eyes of women under black kerchiefs
who chant their god to sleep? They know those were the flowers
hung in His slanting eyes that long night on the cross
His blood congealed to darkness.

'Gold is wrenched from the earth and flesh is made of earth
and I wind hugging both'—

I speak of love,
of that Sun-gendered Queen who bedded with the midnight
    bull
Cretan sea spumed on the sand. Sharp love is not inhaled,
the flesh not fired from shapes without;
it pours to hug the near,
though horned the fruit.
                    I speak of love,
of her who waded with a silent dirge,
bloodless ghost, to lift arches
of a crutched bridge;
of those who screeched back at the goggled owl
to feed old dust-dry mouths and lost their soul,
others, mounting rung by rung the silent ladder
to find a wooden Virgin with a wooden Child.

                    I speak of love,
of shapes that taught the tilted eyes to laugh
untutored hands to touch that sleeping in our sleep
hang like the void beneath a golden mask,
grooves in the spaces of our thoughts
wind in the vast shapelessness of the wind;
of Kings and Queens and Jacks round whom I could not wind,
because, betrayed at birth,
they had no fingers and a paper heart,
beggars of love.
          'Gold is wrenched from the earth
and flesh is made of earth and I wind hugging both.'

Had we not made a promise, you and I,
when the summer gust bumped through whitewashed walls,
that if the clouds rounded fat with rage

35

we would not search for wounded wings
for pomegranate blossom in the street?

Come with me to the gardens you have never seen
where figures cut in green mosaic creep through the fingered
dampness of the leaves—an archaic hunting scene,
half-forgotten battle, ships, delicate ships
winging the dolphin-studded sea;
farewells of stone worn out by ancient feet,
farewells of hearts that still refuse to see
tall ships were built to sail and men to part,
gardens reserved, lit with flowers of glass,
strange blossoms, enamel-throated birds.

And those exclusive blossoms can take root
between back-to-backs where grey washing droops,
if you have touched the wounds of young Adonis
at some Egyptian feast—anemones oleanders—
with open breast chanting your god to sleep,
salt ripples sucked by thin-lipped shells
under the white wounds, gull's wings, white wounds.
Spring breeds such flowers of flashing gold and glass,
white toys that never cry and cannot bleed.

Across the blossoms of my garden—how many shapes,
but not like flowers—a shadow falls,
tall pillars and the walls of a denied house,
where stucco cupids stretch wind-scratched arms
and fractured wings
to touch the light that shafts across their leaves,
glass flowers no fingers ever reach. The eyes
of an imprisoned child still stare out of those windows,
a glass Adonis watching a glass spring.

36

SECOND VOICE
—Wherever I travel toys wound me.
I have seen soldiers, glass soldiers,
fall in scarlet and gold on the field,
was never sure if the wounds were theirs or mine.
They were put to fight again on the same fields
in the same trenches to guard the same pass,
and the hills were a blaze of anemones
and there were broken tanks drowned ships half-pitted graves
lashings of golden broom.
The children had grown up and gone away.

Black-eyes, Nuncle George, the Seraglio, the Hut,
Old Dionysios, the Sticker, merciless hunger
beating-up laughter—strange laughter—
shadows behind the white lit cloth.
The children had grown up and gone away.

And I have heard the boards creaking at night,
sensed the toys were creeping out
to meet their life—
the Black Conjurer up to his fathomless mischief,
the slender Ballerina a swirl of thistledown,
the Little Mermaid cool as a slap of summer spray
floating to gardens of coral, her Prince—
I did not dare turn on the light.
The children had grown up and gone away.

Knitting, knitting, knitting, fingers knitting in desperation,
vests, socks for feet and breasts that are no longer there,

shrouds as endless as Laertes'
lions figured shields blossoms, warriors to be undone at night;
shirts in which the blood of a centaur was knitted
flowing through the needles into the wool.
Did those fingers feel any more?

Beyond that narrow strip of glass how brave the trees;
standing they watched their blossoms fall,
the leaves like red-nosed clowns came tumbling down
and all the wounded green looked on and laughed,
they knew no dawn could break
unless a sun has set.
                    Children in an old man's skin
seated in heated rooms, fearing the cold,
staring at images of subaqueous flowers
painting the ships they hung upon their walls
feeling the humps of paper gargoyles in their books,
their only birds, beaked splashes on the cheek
of china moonlight thin.

Not one of them had dared—the hands were weak—
to grip the topmost branches of the tree
and in a wind of appleblossom sing
like a cicada resurrected from his skin
to snare with frugal song the rising day.
Not one had climbed beyond the mast's crow's nest—
not of an anchored mast that cannot sail—
to scare the cringing gulls and pluck
with both his hands the blue grapes of the sky.
Not one has seized the spire's sharp cross
and scowling at the scowling gargoyles howled
a proud and dangerous song

to break the ghosts that slipped out of their sleep.
They never reached the hawk peak on the hill
to screech back at the storms
until they changed their course.

At Christmas Father Christmas cut in glass
climbs safely up his indoor tree—
spangled with tinsel blobs cotton-wool snow—
to stare up at a frozen star,
no children and no parcels at his feet.
Across his crystal palms the ghosts of gifts,
gifts that are gifts no more.

You remember the double-headed figure in Sienna
under the acute arches of that court
how it smiled and frowned at the lovers,
frowned and smiled at children going hide and seek?
The sculptor sneaked with hammer and chisel
to beat off the wrinkled half—it was a moonless night—
but heard the young head sigh, found the young head's chips
at his feet mixed with the fragments of the bitter half—
an ancient freak
where suffering and joy must share the one stone heart.

Like the charioteer stiff in bronze you stand,
whose chariot horse whip—dust in the wind-whipped dust,
yet stubbornly he clings to stubs of rusty reins
with eyes unbending horn. Your glass toys laugh at you,
    Adonis,
they know, were you to smash them to be free
your heart of glass would break.

39

THIRD VOICE
—Lady of Many Favours, protect
those flowers of glass
flowers and angels of glass
guardians of your image on the altar.

It is hot Sicilian summer,
the dust and flies are hungry,
Lady of Many Favours,
protect your flowers of glass.

From Dormition to Annunciation
your silence is in their silence
in your eyes they look—
Fair it is you should love them—
Patience and unending of glass,
Annunciation to Dormition,
for you to dismiss them.

They are not the weak blossoms,
myrtle lilies the thirty-petalled
roses of your feast-day
that take leave when their flesh is exhausted.

They never answered the wind's voice
that called their brothers out of the earth,
sucked the blood of
no other dawn than your light,
Photophoros, 'Bearer of Light,'
watching through them and beyond
at that Lamp nailed to the cross.

Here, in the dust of your House
they share a dry land's poverty
brittle slaves of an ancient pain.
Protect your flowers of glass,
Lady of Many Favours.

IV

FIRST VOICE
—My toys of glass—soldiers mermaids dancers birds—
I knew I could not freeze their life,
I know they must wander under yellow trees
taste of the cross in ageing mouths.
But with my toys I have tricked the cruel sculptor
my hands are lighter than silver on the leaves
pointing the summer night;
flood of youth leans in my eyes,
glass dawns on Aegean sea
when all the headlands drop their masks of wind
and anchored islands drift like blue triremes.

My toys of glass! some even come silently returning
to glance in my eyes;
there, white in a glass repose,
they find their own shapes once hugged
before urchins and weed crept in their mouths
and scratched the dreaming eyes.
The dimpled stones wait for the runners to return
marble and bronze ablaze like autumn leaves.

And are a glass Adonis' eyes so different from yours?
Do not all eyes see merely shapes desired?

The heart probing the foliage of the wind
gives flesh to all she hoped for
evidence of what was never seen.

If you have glanced at Troy in a ramp of flame
and heard the song of slaves riding the wind,
you can never watch Oedipus searching
out the horror at work in his blood, or
Hamlet, pause of killing and killing die.
You wrench the curtain on the stormy stage
to force the barking darkness into light;
you write the end of every play you see,
cut it where it should stop.
When Adam's fruit, willow root and Judas' tree
mingle their wood, Adonis ripens into glass.
Spring heightens into spring when seen through turning leaves.

Away, over the Aegean, the winds in their season are blowing
foam slashes the nude rock. Howlings
of sunken shapes
cry to the trees:
'What new from the life of the islands?'
'Nothing,' the leaves answer, 'nothing new is born here,
    nothing dies.'
There comes a moment when the tide is poised,
when all that eyes can grip is what has been.
The chariot gritting round the turning-stone
must rush at the goal, the starting-line—
point not singled out by years,
neither by death's long shadow leaning to our feet.
The shapes sidling this way that suck our love,
they turn the head and fix it on the moon.

Then you will see the ships, puffs of canvas cadenced oars
and raging at their poops drums pipes and cymbals,
sailing the land.
The ancient prophecy was true and the city abandoned,
Virgin of the Many Favours weeps.

So for every frame its modicum of love,
and thirsty shapes will suck it to the depth
till like a green vault cistern dry
under some dead imperial church, echoing dead voices.
There and here a pool of dampness clings
to vampire images,
glass-eyed cisterns that quench no thirst.

The heartless and the young they call it lack,
I call it a thesaurus of love this daring gift to the few
of what can never return.
Love is no bandaged cripple trading on our pity.
Through the trampled East he rides an Alexander,
cruel beauty of a disentitled dream.
Are we not cuttings in a comedy of shadows
where here there tomorrow yesterday slide into one,
where what we touch is only a spark of wind,
glass eyes of a glass Adonis our one possession?
Eyes that burn the sand into crystal flowers
solid, whiter than the blossoms of an unseen Isfahan,
glass petals here and ours,
the toys that cannot cry, cannot bleed.
Fire that scorched the sand burns in each crystal drop,
a glass Adonis floats in every cup
and from his lips
the last drop slips of the wine-game to hit the lover's mark.

V

—The flowers that turned my room into a garden—
chrysanthemums carnations gladioli—that first winter died.
I saw their petals harden splinter into crisp dust
thinking I was deceived. But now I know that spring
with blind certainty returns; I have learnt her cruelty
rejoice in her sharp relief laugh at her warning:
'Do not pick an ecstasy that dies'—
as if we had the choice.

Hands ripen into pity, Glass Adonis, to hold what death can
    touch.
Did not that sightless prophet clearly see
the gold-studded Persians would conquer the pass,
yet the King his friend he did not abandon,
did not abandon, but shared his end?
and one man alone carried the magnitude of Rome into her
    death—
the holy ikons wept—an eagle-sandled corpse that blindly led
the slaves in centuries unborn to reach the light.

We were betrayed at birth the Medes had crept behind the pass
before we saw the day, but to fight without rhetoric
that much can not be forbidden.
                              '*Black men tilling black earth,
death suffering their riches,*' but black rejected gifts
make life our own; what god has been so rich?

Forever young always with fertile loins feeding on praise and
    prayer,

44

how poor they lie in their safety how pale in their aloofness!
The Goddess of the Hunt
watching the boy hunter trapped in his purity,
'Weep for the gods,' she cried, 'they cannot even drop a tear
for those they love,' and the death-free stallions of Achilles,
sons of Podagre and the wild West Wind,
like chiselled stone stood mourning, drooping manes,
the charioteer they lost, while Pedasus
mortal Pedasus he shrieked his life away, Patroclus' helper.

One god alone to have the gift of a real giver
rose to the human flesh. Locked on the cross
he offered all for those he loved, his life;
alone, for the angels on guard had run in terror
the sky had closed his eyes.

The fingers of shadow strangling pillars of stone,
pointing where water-birds sing, they bring the temple of life;
they hold the pitcher-bearing maidens and the riding youths
high on the honey-dusted frieze over the statues of the gods.
In every joint of Cyclopean stone, in every fold
of ivory and gold where lions leap and tight-hipped warriors
    fight,
in every gem and bead that firmly hold the frenzied bull
the fawns panting in flight, in all the shadow-trailing spears
that sail the long hexameters to tear
a soft-foot death is sneaking there.

Band after band, spice after spice the priest's hands never
    pause
his fingers never rest winding the binds of gauze,
emollient oils, on flashing limb and breast.

But he cuts out the heart, and with it singing birds
the many words untold cling to a mummy's throat
those cunning hands enfold. Kings hawks wings toys slaves,
pictures on buried walls, lean in a darkness unending
waiting for sun-boats that winged beyond the whiteness of the
    sun.

Nothing then remains of shapes that moved so strangely
through our lives? Nothing but rain and corruption
flooding the doodles of the wind?
                         There is another light.
Lashings of golden flowers down Phaestos' hill
reclining stone and bronze of Attic gods
firm limbs and love-rich lips, they are the seeds
dropped in the staring eyes to teach them how to look,
to search the steeper vistas in the hill-land of the heart.

He had prayed—so he tells us—for years fasted and prayed
in a cell of moonless guilt that leaf-dry Mystic of the City,
when at the peak of night the candle's flame was snuffed,
flame by the ikon of the Virgin of Great Favours.
A storm of whiteness swooped into his cell
sharper than all the diamonds polished by the sun,
blinding burning purging,
it hung on the walls its dancing jewels,
The True Fire of Love.
                     Oil that fed it was charity—
so he tells us—the wick the spirit. Flesh suffering the years,
where had they gone? His limbs eagle-down light, his eyes
full of that double sunrise in the heart and in the cell.
Away it flashed sudden as coming that storm of light,
and dark poured back into the hermit's heart—he tells us—

like waves in the rift of a sinking ship.
But kneeling dry to his prayers an afterglow gilded his eyes,
his heart, his wrinkled heart was light,
lighter than starred apple-bloom riding the wind.

And I who never fasted and who never prayed
have seen that light. It swept from eyes of Spanish blue,
the oil was cruelty the wick was scorn.
Young years of loneliness had fed that flame
wild like the message from crag to hill-head
that forced the Old Ones, guilt, to become guests
and not the hosts of death. Love the tamer
can ripen in the wind of hate.
Have you felt with your hands on the rock
the ghost of that hoof?

Only because you loved me so wide-heartedly
I reached to touch the whiteness of that light;
no Alexander at the navel of black Babylon
no Bulgar-killer at the Golden Gates
have felt such exaltation, such security
as I beside your feet, at your home.

Because you loved me so unflinchingly those faithless swallows
filled the winter eaves, December hills were green like dancing
peacocks and gold thread stitched the dead October leaves.
Only because you loved me all is charged with day
and in a world that does not know fulfillment
my life has been fulfilled—
you who strangely faded in the sunset
leaf-simple as the grass, because you loved me so unsparingly
I now can live without a spring of glass.